Metal Detecting for Kids

An Easy Guide for Finding Buried Treasures With a Metal Detector

By Mark Smith

ISBN-13: 978-1503033221
ISBN-10: 1503033228
Metal Detecting for Kids: An Easy Guide for Finding Buried Treasures With a Metal Detector

Table of Contents

An Old Treasure Legend

Years ago there was a mysterious pirate who hid large amounts of treasure all over the world. He was very careful and very quiet about where and how he hid his treasure. You see, this pirate was smarter than all the other pirates out there. He knew that if he hid all of his treasure in one place, it would only take one person to find it all. No, no, no! That must never happen.

This pirate was different. He didn't want just one person finding his treasure. He wanted lots of people finding it. This is a pirate that actually wanted to share his treasure. Weird, right? But there was a reason he did this. He wanted to share the fun. He wanted people like **YOU** to be part of the adventure. Just imagine how much fun it would be to dig up your very own treasure!

So instead of stuffing his mountain of treasure into an old wooden chest and burying it deep under the sand of some long forgotten island, this pirate decided he would hide a coin here and a coin there. He spread his huge pile of treasure all over the world.

He was very sneaky about it too. He would wait until the sun set, and only then would he hide his prized treasure. He used the cover of night to hide in the shadows so no one would see him.

Being seen hiding the treasure would just make things too easy for all the eager treasure hunters out there, and the great sense of adventure would be lost. He had to keep every single treasure location a secret.

He has been doing this for years. In fact, he is still hiding treasure right now as you read this book, and here's the really cool part. You get to go outside and find some of this treasure. You get to be part of the adventure and all you need is your new trusty metal detector to do it. This sounds like lots of fun doesn't it? Wait because it gets even better.

Not only will you be able to find some of this mysterious pirate's long lost treasure, but you will be able to find all sorts of other treasures as well.

There are millions of pieces of treasure hidden out there. These treasures could be a simple penny, a meteorite from outer space or a giant gold nugget and guess what? They are all waiting for you to find them. Let's go find some treasure!

Don't Forget!

Before you go out and start digging up lots of treasure, there are a few things that you must always remember.

Ask Your Parents First

Always ask your parents for permission before you go treasure hunting. It is too easy to get excited and wander off. Let your parents know where you will be and where you are going.

Never Go Treasure Hunting Alone

Always go treasure hunting with a partner. Your parents

would be the best choice. If they can't go, then go with a friend.

Private Property
Don't go treasure hunting on private property without permission. This includes your neighbor's yard. If you want to hunt for treasure on private property, then you must ask for permission first.

Don't Be Destructive

Don't destroy stuff when you are trying to recover your treasure. Trees, buildings, plants and yards must look exactly like they did before you started hunting for treasure. Save the destruction for games like Minecraft.

Fill In Your Holes

It can be really easy to forget to fill in your holes when you pull a shiny piece of treasure out of the ground. Always fill in your holes. It should look like you were never even there!

Smaller Holes Are Better

Digging a huge hole can be a lot of fun, but filling in a huge hole is not. When you locate a piece of treasure, try to dig a small hole.

Throw Away Trash

People have been throwing their trash on the ground for hundreds of years. You will be finding a lot of this trash when you go treasure hunting. If you dig up a piece of trash, don't throw it back in the hole. Take it with you and throw it away.

Be Careful!

Your piece of treasure could be an old rusty piece of metal, a sharp piece of glass or a deadly snake! Always be extra careful when you are treasure hunting. This is why it is very important to always make sure an adult is with you.

Get To Know Your Metal Detector

Every metal detector looks a little different, but they all do pretty much the same thing. They help you find treasure. That's the really awesome part. Some metal detectors can even tell you what the treasure might be before you start digging it up!

The very first thing you need to do is read the instruction manual that came with your metal detector. It will tell you how to put your metal detector together. It will also tell you what all the knobs and buttons do. You may even want to have your parents help you with this part. The more you understand what your metal detector is trying to tell you, the better you will be at finding treasure.

It also helps to understand what each part of the metal detector is used for. Let's take a closer look.

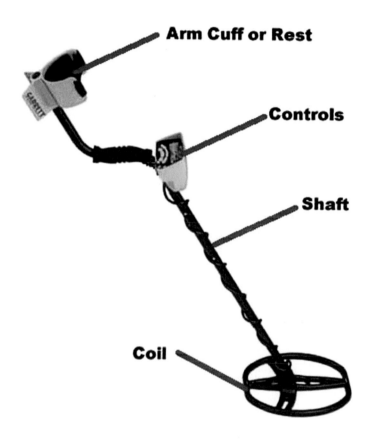

Arm Cuff or Rest

Controls

Shaft

Coil

Metal detectors have a lot of pieces don't they? Don't worry, it's easy to understand what each piece does. Let's start at the top and work our way down.

The Arm Rest

This is where you rest your arm. Your arm rest might even have a strap to hold your arm in place while you are using your metal detector.

The Controls
This is the command center for your metal detector. This is where you can make changes to how your metal detector works. Your instruction manual will be able to tell you the best way to set everything up.

Your metal detector might also have some sort of visual identification on the controls that help tell you what a piece of treasure is before you dig it up. Pretty fancy huh?

The Shaft
This is the long skinny part that holds the coil. On some metal detectors, you can adjust the length of the shaft. Have your parents help you with this part. Your metal detector should be easy to swing and it should be comfortable.

The Coil
The coil is one of the most important parts of the metal detector. You use it to scan the ground in front of you, but you have to be careful using it. If you swing it too fast, you might miss some treasure. It is best to keep the coil as close to the ground as possible and move it nice and slow.

That's all there is to it! Let's go find some treasure!

Where Should You Start?

Start hunting for treasure right in your very own yard! This will be the perfect place to learn how to use your metal detector, and you never know what you may find. Once you have searched your entire yard, you can start searching some other great places. Here are some of the best places to find treasure. Make sure metal detecting is allowed before you go!

- The Park
- The Playground
- School
- Sports Fields
- The Beach
- Campgrounds
- Picnic Areas
- Churches

You will be able to find treasure any place where people have been!

The Right Way to Use Your Metal Detector

Believe it or not, there is a right way and a wrong way to use your new metal detector. If you use your metal detector the wrong way, you won't find as much treasure. So let's make sure we are doing things the right way!

Slow and Steady

Start off by going nice and slow. Move the coil slowly over the ground from the left to the right. Metal detecting is not a race. You want to scan every inch or centimeter of ground with your coil. Try to imagine you are painting the ground with your coil. Don't miss anything.

As you move forward, slowly swing your coil from the left to the right like the image below.

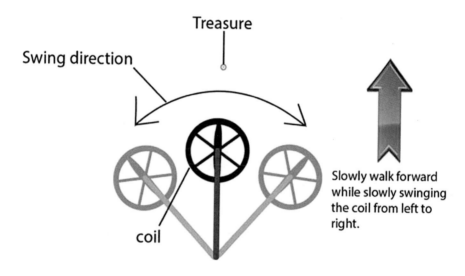

Treasure

Swing direction

coil

Slowly walk forward while slowly swinging the coil from left to right.

Keep Your Coil Close to the Ground

Don't scrape the ground with your coil and don't hold it too high off the ground. Keep the coil close to the ground at all times. Try to avoid bumping your coil on rocks, sticks and trees too.

As you use the coil to search for treasure, keep it level at all times. Look at the image below. This is the perfect way to swing your coil.

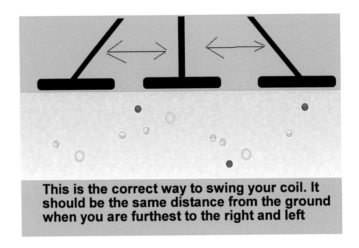

This is the correct way to swing your coil. It should be the same distance from the ground when you are furthest to the right and left

Look at the image below. This is the wrong way to swing your coil.

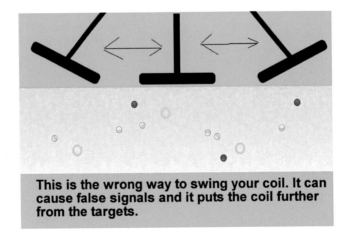

This is the wrong way to swing your coil. It can cause false signals and it puts the coil further from the targets.

Practice makes perfect! Practice walking slowly and swinging your metal detector coil at the same time. With a little bit of practice, you will be swinging your metal detector like a pro!

How Do You Know When You Have Found Treasure?
Pay attention to your metal detector as you move the coil from left to right. When the coil passes over some treasure, your metal detector should make a noise. Your metal detector may also have a small display screen that helps you identify what and how deep your treasure is.

Now that you have found a piece of treasure, let's see if we can pinpoint its exact location under the ground.

Pinpoint

Remember when I said digging a big hole is not a good idea? Pinpointing your treasure helps you get a better idea of where your treasure is. This way you don't have to dig a huge hole. You can just dig a very small hole to get to your treasure.

Your metal detector might have a special mode or feature that helps you pinpoint your treasure. Look over your instruction manual to see if it does.

Pinpointing is very easy once you get the hang of it. You will be using your eyes and your ears as a team. As you move your coil from left to right, listen to the sound your metal detector makes when it passes over the treasure.

As you are doing this, watch the coil very closely. When your metal detector makes a sound, it is directly over the treasure. Your eyes and your ears will be working as a team to help you locate the exact spot where the treasure is buried.

When you think you know exactly where the treasure is, slowly move your coil back and forth over the spot. Instead of making wide swings from left to right, slowly make your swings smaller and smaller until you know exactly where the treasure is buried. Look at this picture below. It will make it easier to understand how to become a master at pinpointing.

Use smaller swings

Treasure

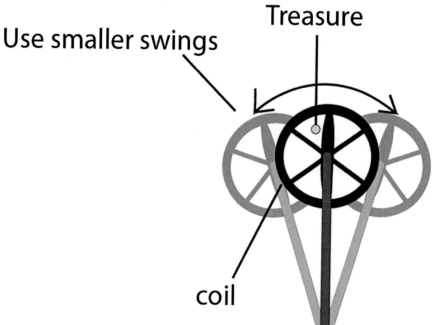

coil

Let's Get That Treasure!

Finally! The moment we have all been waiting for. Let's get that piece of treasure out of the ground and see what it is! This is the exciting part, but you have to be careful. What if your treasure is very old and rare? You don't want to damage it, so we have to try and get it out of the ground carefully. Here is the best way to get that treasure safely out of the ground.

Keep your eyes on the spot where you think the treasure is buried. Using a shovel or a hand held digging tool, carefully dig a circle around the buried treasure like the picture below. This is called cutting a plug.

Once you have completely cut a circle around your buried treasure, gently lift the plug up by pressing down on the handle of your digging tool. Be careful not to break or bend it. Look at the picture below.

Now you should be able to easily lift the plug you cut out of the ground like the picture below.

Where is the treasure? It might still be in the hole or it could be in the plug. Use your metal detector to check them both.

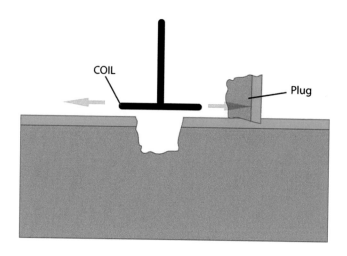

Scan the hole with your metal detector, then scan the plug.

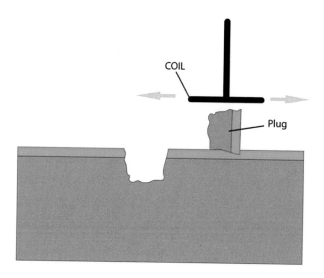

If your metal detector makes a sound when you swing it over the hole, your treasure is still buried. You have to carefully keep digging to find it. Using your shovel, remove a small amount of dirt and scan it with your metal detector until you locate your new piece of treasure. Don't let your shovel get in the way. If it is made from metal, it will cause your metal detector to go crazy!

If your metal detector makes a sound when you swing it over the plug, then you can carefully break apart the plug until you find your treasure.

Sometimes there might be one, two, three or hundreds of pieces of treasure in the same hole. Always make sure you double check the hole after you have removed a piece of treasure. There could always be more.

Once you have found your piece of treasure, make sure to put everything back the way it was. Fill in your hole and take any trash you may have found with you. That's all there is to it. Finding treasure with a metal detector is simple, easy and tons of fun. Now get out there and start finding your own treasure.

Thanks!

Thanks for purchasing my book. If you enjoyed Metal Detecting for Kids, then leave a review. I would really appreciate it.

If you want even more tips on how you can find even more treasure, then I highly suggest you read my best selling book entitled:

Metal Detecting: A Guide to Mastering the Greatest Hobby In the World.

It is a little more advanced, but it is loaded with invaluable information. Over 200 pages of facts, tips and illustrations. It is available in both digital and print.

People find great treasures every single day with their metal detectors. If you want to see some of the best treasures found with a metal detector then you have got to check out my book called:

Incredible Metal Detecting Discoveries.

This book is packed full of some of the greatest treasure stories on the planet!

You don't always need a metal detector to find old valuable

coins made from gold and silver. They could be right under your nose. Learn the EASY way to find old coins in my best selling book entitled:

Coin Hunting Made Easy

It is available in digital format and paperback.

Drop me a line and let me know how you are doing out there. I always love hearing about things that other people are finding. You can email me at: wordsaremything@gmail.com

Happy hunting,
Mark Smith

Made in the USA
Middletown, DE
09 January 2015